About This Book

Title: *Night Flight*

Step: 5

Word Count: 198

Skills in Focus: Long vowel i spelled y and igh

Tricky Words: animals, during, where, claws, dark, find, sound, comes, bother, people

Ideas For Using This Book

Before Reading:
- **Comprehension:** Look at the title and cover image together. Walk through the pictures in the book with readers and have them make predictions about what they might learn while reading. Help them make connections by asking what they already know about bats.
- **Accuracy:** Practice saying the tricky words listed on page 1.
- **Phonics:** Tell students they will read words with the long vowel patterns *igh* and *y*. Explain that *igh* and *y* can make the long vowel sound /i/. Have students look at the title of this book, *Night Flight*. Ask readers to point to the vowel patterns in the title. Help them practice blending the sounds in *night* and *flight*. Have students take a quick look through the first few pages of text to identify and decode additional words with long /i/ sounds spelled with *igh* and *y*.

During Reading:
- Have readers point under each word as they read it.
- **Decoding:** If readers are stuck on a word, help them say each sound and blend the sounds together smoothly. Be sure to point out words with *igh* and *y* vowel patterns as they appear.
- **Comprehension:** Invite readers to talk about new things they are learning about bats while reading. What are they learning that they didn't know before?

After Reading:
Discuss the book. Some ideas for questions:
- Where and when do you think you might see a bat flying? Would you be afraid to see a bat?
- What do you still wonder about bats?

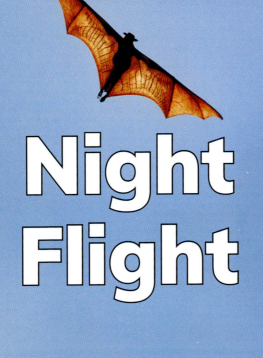

Night Flight

Text by Marley Richmond

Reading Consultant
Deborah MacPhee, PhD
Professor, School of Teaching and Learning
Illinois State University

PICTURE WINDOW BOOKS
a capstone imprint

Bats are animals that can fly in the sky.

Bats sleep during the day when it is bright.

They fly by night when it is dark.

Bats might sleep in caves or other places where it is not too bright.

Caves are not bright, even when the sun is in the sky.

Bats hang from their claws when they sleep. They hang on tight!

Flying

Twilight is the time between day and night.

At twilight, bats take flight.

Bats fly in the dark sky.

They look for food.

Eating

Lots of bats eat bugs.
Bats can catch bugs as they fly.

But bats do not find bugs with their sight.

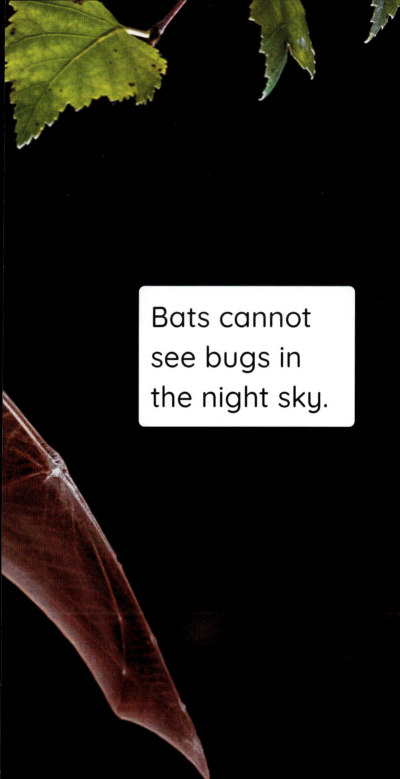

Bats cannot see bugs in the night sky.

They do not use light to see at night.

Bats use sound to find bugs at night.

Bats make clicks. The sound goes out and then comes back.

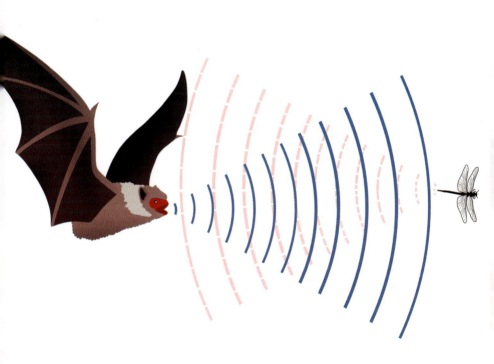

The clicks tell bats where bugs are in the night sky.

Lights

Bats do not like bright light.

Some lights people use are too bright for bats.

Lights on the street and in homes might bother bats nearby.

Bats give some people a fright. But bats just like to fly by night.

More Ideas:

Phonics Activity

Matching Vowel Patterns:
Prepare word cards with vowel patterns. Patterns could include *igh* or *y*. Place the cards on a workspace. Ask readers to make pairs of words that use the same vowel pattern to make the long /i/ sound. Have readers sound out each pair of words and compare the long vowel sounds each vowel pattern makes.

Suggested words:
- *y*: fly, sky, by, nearby
- *igh*: bright, night, tight, twilight, flight, sight, light, might, fright

Extended Learning Activity

Write a Story:
Ask readers to choose an animal and imagine how they would spend one day as that animal. Where and when would they sleep? What kind of food would they eat and how would they find it? Would they see people? Would the people bother them? Challenge readers to use words with long /i/ vowel sounds spelled with *igh* or *y*.

Published by Picture Window Books, an imprint of Capstone
1710 Roe Crest Drive, North Mankato, Minnesota 56003
capstonepub.com

Copyright © 2026 by Capstone.
All rights reserved. No part of this publication may be reproduced in whole or in part, or stored in a retrieval system, or transmitted in any form or by any means, electronic, mechanical, photocopying, recording, or otherwise, without written permission of the publisher.

Library of Congress Cataloging-in-Publication Data is available on the Library of Congress website.

ISBN: 9798875227196 (hardback)
ISBN: 9798875230929 (paperback)
ISBN: 9798875230905 (eBook PDF)

Image Credits: iStock: Antagain, 22–23 (mosquito), CreativeNature_nl, 26, milan noga, 28–29, milehightraveler, 30–31, Paul Colley, 18–19, RebeccaBloomPhoto, 24, tane-mahuta, cover; Shutterstock: All-stock-photos, 8–9, Artazum, 27, ATTILA Barsan, 11, FJAH, 1, 14–15, kajornyot wildlife photography, 4–5, 32, Memo Ossa, 22–23 (bat), Miroslav Srb, 7, OSTILL is Franck Camhi, 2–3, Phoenix Expeditions, 6, Rudmer Zwerver, 16–17, 20–21, SaskiaAcht, 10, Watthana Tirahimonchan, 25, wimammoth, 12–13

Printed and bound in China. 6274